Mushroom

A mouthwatering medley of delightful dishes

Lesley Mackley

This is a Parragon Publishing Book
First published in 2004

Parragon Publishing
Queen Street House
4 Queen Street
Bath
BA1 1HE
United Kingdom

ISBN: 1-40542-954-2

Printed in Indonesia

Produced by the BRIDGEWATER BOOK COMPANY LTD

Photographer: Karen Thomas
Prop Stylist: Karen Thomas
Food Stylist: Valerie Berry

Note
This book uses imperial, metric, or US cup measurements. Follow the
same units of measurement throughout; do not mix imperial and metric.
All spoon measurements are level: teaspoons are assumed to be 5 ml,
and tablespoons are assumed to be 15 ml. Unless otherwise stated, milk
is assumed to be whole, eggs and individual vegetables such as potatoes are medium, and
pepper is freshly ground black pepper.

The times given are an approximate guide only. The preparation times may differ according
to the techniques used by different people and the cooking times may vary as a result of the
type of oven used.

Recipes using raw or very lightly cooked eggs should be avoided by infants, the elderly,
pregnant women, convalescents, and anyone suffering from
an illness. Pregnant and breastfeeding women are advised to avoid eating peanuts and
peanut products.

Contents

Introduction

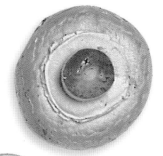

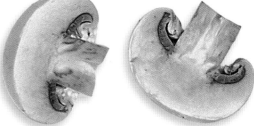

IT IS DIFFICULT *to think of any other vegetables which are as versatile as mushrooms. Bake, pan-fry, or broil them, or eat them raw. Wrap them in pastry, add to stir-fries, toss into salads, sprinkle over pizzas, stir into pasta sauces, or add them to soups. Serve for breakfast, lunch, or supper, or as cocktail snacks and appetizers. They add a "meaty" texture to vegetarian dishes, and can form a vital part of a healthy diet. Mushrooms contain vitamins and minerals, they are low in calories, and they contain virtually no fat, sugar, or salt.*

Choose from white or brown mushrooms, ranging in size from tiny whites to large saucers. Alternatively, you can select from exotic varieties such as pretty oyster mushrooms, which are delicate and require little cooking, or the more chewy shiitakes, which are ideal for Asian dishes. Then there are large, coarse

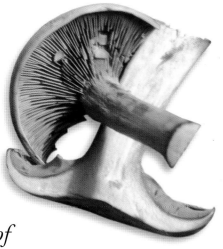

horse mushrooms; fragrant, blue-tinted blewits; nuttily flavored puffball mushrooms; or the tiny, long-stemmed enokis, which are so suitable for salads and stir-fries. Don't forget the possibilities of dried mushrooms, which will keep for ages and add a wonderfully intense flavor when used in combination with fresh mushrooms.

You can store mushrooms in a paper bag in the salad drawer of the refrigerator for up to five days. Prepacked mushrooms do not require washing, but you should rinse loose ones just before use. Remember that the stalks and skins are delicious as well as nutritious, so there is no need for you to remove them.

The best thing about mushrooms is that they are available to add taste and variety to your recipes all the year round.

Chinese Mushroom Soup

The combination of dried and fresh mushrooms gives a particularly intense flavor to this light soup.

1 Bring the water to a boil in a large pan. Remove the pan from the heat and add the shiitake mushrooms. Let soak for 10 minutes, then remove the mushrooms with a slotted spoon, chop coarsely, and set aside until required. Strain the mushroom liquid to remove any dirt or grit and pour into a clean pan.

2 Add the stock to the mushroom liquid and bring to a boil. Add the ginger, garlic, shiitake, and cremini mushrooms and soy sauce. Cover and let simmer for 10 minutes.

3 Meanwhile, soak the noodles in a bowl of hot water for 10 minutes, or according to the package instructions. Drain, add to the soup, and let simmer for an additional 3 minutes.

4 Sprinkle the scallions over the soup and garnish with the chopped cilantro. Transfer to individual bowls and serve.

SERVES 4

PREPARATION TIME: 10 MINUTES, PLUS 10 MINUTES SOAKING

COOKING TIME: 15 MINUTES

$^2/_3$ cup water

$^1/_4$ cup dried shiitake mushrooms

4 cups vegetable or chicken stock

1$^1/_4$-inch/3-cm piece fresh gingerroot, grated

2 garlic cloves, thinly sliced

3 oz/85 g fresh cremini mushrooms, thickly sliced

1 tbsp soy sauce

2$^1/_2$ oz/70 g rice vermicelli noodles

3 scallions, thinly sliced

chopped fresh cilantro, to garnish

Creamy Mushroom & Tarragon Soup

SERVES 4–6

PREPARATION TIME: 10 MINUTES

COOKING TIME: 35 MINUTES

3 heaping tbsp butter

1 onion, chopped

1 lb 9 oz/700 g white mushrooms, coarsely chopped

3¹/₂ cups vegetable stock

3 tbsp chopped fresh tarragon, plus extra to garnish

²/₃ cup sour cream

salt and pepper

You may prefer to use heavy cream as an alternative to sour cream in this sumptuous soup.

1 Melt half the butter in a large pan. Add the onion and cook gently for 10 minutes, until soft. Add the remaining butter and the mushrooms and stir-fry for 5 minutes, or until the mushrooms are browned.

2 Stir in the stock and tarragon, bring to a boil, then reduce the heat and let simmer gently for 20 minutes. Transfer to a food processor or blender and process until smooth. Return the soup to the pan.

3 Stir in the sour cream and add salt and pepper to taste. Reheat the soup gently until hot. Ladle into warmed serving bowls and garnish with chopped tarragon. Serve at once.

Mushroom Bruschetta

SERVES 4

PREPARATION TIME: 10 MINUTES

COOKING TIME: 10 MINUTES

12 slices French baguette, each
    ¹/₂ inch/1 cm thick, or 2 individual
    French baguettes, cut lengthwise

3 tbsp olive oil

2 garlic cloves, crushed

8 oz/225 g cremini mushrooms, sliced

8 oz/225 g mixed wild mushrooms

2 tsp lemon juice

salt and pepper

2 tbsp chopped fresh parsley

These bruschetta can be served as an accompaniment to drinks, as an appetizer or as a snack at any time.

1 Preheat the broiler to medium. Toast the bread under the hot broiler until golden on both sides. Keep warm.

2 Meanwhile, heat the oil in a skillet. Add the garlic and cook gently for a few seconds, then add the cremini mushrooms. Cook, stirring constantly, over high heat for 3 minutes. Add the wild mushrooms and cook for an additional 2 minutes. Stir in the lemon juice.

3 Season to taste with salt and pepper and stir in the chopped parsley.

4 Spoon the mushroom mixture onto the hot toast and serve.

Scrambled Eggs with Chanterelles

SERVES 2–3

PREPARATION TIME: 5 MINUTES

COOKING TIME: 8 MINUTES

4 oz/115 g fresh chanterelles or morels

3 tbsp butter

4 large eggs

1 tbsp milk

2 tbsp snipped fresh chives

salt and pepper

2–3 slices buttered toast, to serve

The delicate flavor of chanterelles goes particularly well with eggs, but any small wild mushrooms may be used instead.

1 Rinse the chanterelles under cold running water and let drain on paper towels. Melt half the butter in a large, heavy-bottom pan. Add the chanterelles and cook, stirring frequently, for 2–3 minutes. Remove the chanterelles from the pan and let drain on paper towels until required.

2 Whisk the eggs and milk together in a bowl. Melt the remaining butter in the pan. Stir in the egg mixture and cook very gently, stirring constantly, until lightly set.

3 Stir in the chanterelles and chives. Season to taste with salt and pepper, then divide between the slices of buttered toast and serve at once. As an attractive and fun alternative, set aside the eggshells, rinse under running water, and spoon the cooked scrambled egg and chanterelles mixture into the shells before serving.

Hot-&-Sour Noodle & Mushroom Salad

Chili sauces vary in strength, so add the sauce to this salad's dressing a little at a time.

1 Soak the noodles in a bowl of hot water for 10 minutes, or according to the package instructions. Drain and place in a large bowl. Add the sesame oil and toss until the noodles are coated with the oil.

2 Slice the scallions and mushrooms, then cut the cucumber into short thin sticks. Add to the noodles in the bowl.

3 To make the dressing, place the sesame oil, fish sauce, lime juice, sugar, and chili sauce in a small bowl and whisk together. Stir in the chopped cilantro.

4 Pour the dressing over the salad and toss until coated. Serve at once.

SERVES 4

PREPARATION TIME: 10 MINUTES, PLUS 10 MINUTES SOAKING

COOKING TIME: NONE

9 oz/250 g rice vermicelli noodles

2 tbsp sesame oil

6 scallions

6 oz/175 g white mushrooms

1/2 cucumber

Dressing

4 tbsp sesame oil

2 tbsp Thai fish sauce

juice of 2 limes

1 tsp sugar

1–2 tsp hot chili sauce

2 tbsp chopped fresh cilantro

Warm Mushroom, Spinach & Pancetta Salad

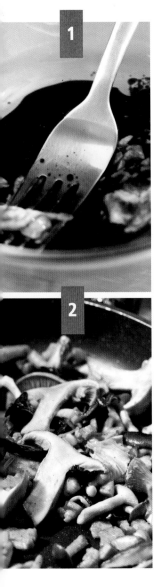

Pancetta cubetti is ready prepared cubes of pancetta, available in packages. If unavailable, cut the pancetta or bacon slices into cubes.

1 To make the dressing, place the olive oil, vinegar, mustard, sugar, salt, and pepper in a small bowl and whisk together. Rinse the baby spinach under cold running water, then drain and place in a large salad bowl.

2 Heat the oil in a large skillet. Add the pancetta and cook for 3 minutes. Add the mushrooms and cook for 3–4 minutes, or until tender.

3 Pour the dressing into the skillet and immediately turn the cooked mixture and dressing into the bowl with the spinach. Toss until coated with the dressing and serve at once.

SERVES 4

PREPARATION TIME: 5 MINUTES

COOKING TIME: 8 MINUTES

generous 6 cups fresh baby
    spinach leaves

2 tbsp olive oil

5¹/₂ oz/150 g pancetta cubetti

10 oz/280 g mixed wild mushrooms,
    sliced

Dressing

5 tbsp olive oil

1 tbsp balsamic vinegar

1 tsp Dijon mustard

pinch of sugar

salt and pepper

Linguine with Wild Mushroom & Mascarpone Sauce

This simple sauce could be served with any dried or fresh pasta.

1 Slice the mushrooms. Cook the pasta in a large pan of lightly salted boiling water for 10–12 minutes, or according to the package instructions, until tender but still firm to the bite.

2 Meanwhile, melt the butter in a separate large pan. Add the garlic and sliced mushrooms and cook for 3–4 minutes.

3 Reduce the heat and stir in the mascarpone cheese, milk, and sage. Season to taste with salt and pepper.

4 Drain the pasta thoroughly and add to the mushroom sauce. Toss until the pasta is well coated with the sauce. Transfer to warmed dishes and serve at once with freshly grated Parmesan cheese.

SERVES 4

PREPARATION TIME: 5 MINUTES

COOKING TIME: 10 MINUTES

8 oz/225 g mixed wild mushrooms

1 lb/450 g dried linguine

salt and pepper

2 oz/55 g butter

1 garlic clove, crushed

generous 1 cup mascarpone cheese

2 tbsp milk

1 tsp chopped fresh sage

freshly grated Parmesan cheese,
    to serve

Mushroom Brioches

PREPARATION TIME: 15 MINUTES

COOKING TIME: 25 MINUTES

6 small brioches

5 tbsp olive oil

1 garlic clove, crushed

2 shallots, finely chopped

12 oz/350 g cremini mushrooms, sliced

1 tsp Dijon mustard

2 tbsp dry sherry

1 tsp chopped fresh thyme

$^2/_3$ cup heavy cream

salt and pepper

These mushroom-filled brioches can be served as an appetizer or a light lunch.

1 Preheat the oven to 400°F/200°C. Cut the tops off the brioches and scoop out the insides of each one to make a hollow case. Brush the insides of the brioches with 3 tablespoons of the oil. Place them on a baking sheet and cook in the oven for 10–12 minutes, until crisp.

2 Meanwhile, heat the remaining oil in a pan. Add the garlic and shallots and cook for 3 minutes, until soft. Add the mushrooms and cook gently for 5 minutes, stirring occasionally.

3 Stir in the mustard, sherry, thyme, cream, and salt and pepper to taste, then cook for a few minutes until the mixture is slightly reduced and thickened. Spoon into the brioche cases and serve at once.

Mushroom & Goat Cheese Frittata

PREPARATION TIME: 5 MINUTES

COOKING TIME: 15 MINUTES

4 large eggs

2 tbsp cold water

pepper

7 oz/200 g goat cheese log

4 tbsp olive oil

8 oz/225 g large mushrooms,
    thinly sliced

2 garlic cloves, finely chopped

2 tbsp chopped fresh parsley

A frittata is an Italian version of a Spanish omelet. It makes a great lunch dish with salad and bread.

1 Preheat the broiler to medium. Beat the eggs and water together in a small bowl and season to taste with pepper. Remove the rind from the cheese and cut into cubes.

2 Heat the oil in a 7-inch/18-cm diameter omelet pan or skillet with a heatproof handle. Add the mushrooms and garlic and cook until the mushrooms are starting to crisp at the edges.

3 Pour the beaten eggs over the mushrooms and cook over low heat for 3 minutes, until set underneath.

4 Sprinkle the cubes of goat cheese on top of the frittata and place the omelet pan under the hot broiler until the eggs are set and the cheese is starting to melt. Sprinkle with chopped parsley, then cut into wedges and serve at once.

Mixed Mushroom Pizza

Using ready-made bases makes these pizzas quick and easy to assemble.

1 Preheat the oven to 475°F/240°C. Mix 2 tablespoons of the oil, the garlic, and oregano together and brush over the pizza bases.

2 Mix the curd cheese and milk together in a bowl. Season to taste with salt and pepper and spread the mixture over the pizza bases, leaving a 1¹/₂-inch/ 4-cm border.

3 Heat the butter and remaining oil together in a large skillet. Add the mushrooms and cook over high heat for 2 minutes. Remove the skillet from the heat, season to taste with salt and pepper, and stir in the lemon juice and marjoram.

4 Spoon the mushroom mixture over the pizza bases, leaving a ¹/₂-inch/1-cm border. Sprinkle with the grated Parmesan cheese, then bake in the oven for 12–15 minutes, until the crusts are crisp and the mushrooms are cooked. Serve at once.

MAKES 2 X 9-INCH/ 23-CM PIZZAS

PREPARATION TIME: 10 MINUTES
COOKING TIME: 17 MINUTES

3 tbsp oil

2 garlic cloves, crushed

2 tbsp chopped fresh oregano

2 x 9-inch/23-cm ready-made thin and crispy pizza bases

³/₄ cup curd cheese

1 tbsp milk

salt and pepper

3 tbsp butter

12 oz/350 g mixed mushrooms, sliced

2 tsp lemon juice

1 tbsp chopped fresh marjoram

4 tbsp freshly grated Parmesan cheese

Portobello Mushrooms Stuffed with Spinach & Bacon

SERVES 4

PREPARATION TIME: 15 MINUTES

COOKING TIME: 30 MINUTES

---

5 cups fresh baby spinach leaves

4 portobello mushrooms

3 tbsp olive oil

2 oz/55 g rindless bacon, finely diced

2 garlic cloves, crushed

1 cup fresh white or brown
   bread crumbs

2 tbsp chopped fresh basil

salt and pepper

For a vegetarian dish you could omit the bacon and use sundried tomatoes instead.

1 Preheat the oven to 400°F/200°C. Rinse the spinach and place in a pan with only the water clinging to the leaves. Cook for 2–3 minutes, until wilted. Drain, squeezing out as much liquid as possible, and chop finely. Cut the stalks from the mushrooms and chop finely, reserving the whole caps.

2 Heat 2 tablespoons of the oil in a skillet. Add the mushroom caps, rounded-side down, and cook for 1 minute. Remove from the skillet and arrange, rounded-side down, in a large ovenproof dish.

3 Add the chopped mushroom stalks, bacon, and garlic to the skillet and cook for 5 minutes. Stir in the spinach, bread crumbs, basil, and salt and pepper to taste. Mix well and divide the stuffing between the mushroom caps.

4 Drizzle the remaining oil over the top and bake in the oven for 20 minutes, until crisp and golden.

Mushroom & Provolone Kabobs

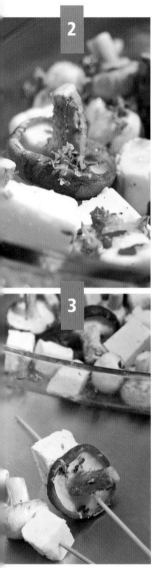

These kabobs taste particularly good cooked on a barbecue, but they are also delicious cooked under the broiler.

1 To make the marinade, mix the lemon zest and juice, olive oil, thyme, chili, salt, and pepper together in a small bowl.

2 Place the shiitake and white mushrooms in a large bowl. Cut the provolone cheese into 1-inch/2.5-cm cubes and add to the mushrooms. Pour over the marinade and toss gently to coat evenly. Cover with plastic wrap and let marinate in the refrigerator for 2 hours.

3 Preheat the barbecue or broiler. Thread the marinated mushrooms and provolone cheese onto 4 metal or presoaked wooden skewers, reserving any remaining marinade for basting.

4 Cook the kabobs over medium–hot coals or under the broiler for 10 minutes, turning and basting frequently with the marinade. Serve at once.

SERVES 4

PREPARATION TIME: 10 MINUTES, PLUS 2 HOURS MARINATING

COOKING TIME: 10 MINUTES

16 fresh shiitake mushrooms, about 4 oz/115 g

16 white mushrooms, about 8 oz/225 g

12 oz/350 g provolone cheese

Marinade

zest and juice of 2 small lemons

2 tbsp olive oil

2 tbsp chopped fresh thyme

small fresh red chili, seeded and finely chopped

salt and pepper

Mushroom Burgers

Even committed carnivores will love these tasty burgers!

1 Place the mushrooms in a food processor and process briefly until chopped.

2 Heat 4 tablespoons of the oil and the butter in a large skillet. Add the shallots and cook for 5 minutes, until soft. Add the chopped mushrooms and cook, stirring frequently, for 5 minutes.

3 Let the mixture cool, then stir in the mustard, tarragon, bread crumbs, and salt and pepper to taste. Mix well, then divide the mixture into 6 portions and shape into patties. Let chill for 1 hour.

4 Preheat the broiler to medium. Heat the remaining oil in the skillet. Add the burgers, in batches if necessary, and cook for 5 minutes on each side until golden and cooked through. Split the burger buns in half. Toast the cut sides of the burger buns under the hot broiler, then butter lightly. Serve the burgers in the buns with lettuce and mustard.

SERVES 6

PREPARATION TIME: 10 MINUTES, PLUS 1 HOUR CHILLING

COOKING TIME: 20 MINUTES

1 lb 9 oz/700 g mixed flat and cremini mushrooms

8 tbsp olive oil

2 oz/55 g butter

4 shallots, finely chopped

1 tsp Dijon mustard

1 tbsp chopped fresh tarragon

4 cups fresh brown bread crumbs

salt and pepper

6 burger buns

butter, for spreading

To serve

lettuce leaves

tarragon mustard

Mushroom & Bean Chili

Serve this delicious chili with plain boiled rice and sour cream.

1 Heat 1 tablespoon of the oil in a large skillet. Add the mushrooms and stir-fry until golden. Remove with a slotted spoon and set aside until required.

2 Add the remaining oil to the skillet. Add the onion, garlic, and green bell pepper and cook for 5 minutes. Stir in the paprika, coriander, cumin, and chili powder and cook for an additional 1 minute.

3 Add the tomatoes, stock, and tomato paste, stir well, then cover and let cook for 20 minutes.

4 Add the reserved mushrooms and kidney beans and cook, covered, for an additional 20 minutes. Season to taste with salt and pepper and stir in the cilantro. Serve at once.

SERVES 6

PREPARATION TIME: 10 MINUTES

COOKING TIME: 50 MINUTES

4 tbsp olive oil

8 oz/225 g small white mushrooms

1 large onion, chopped

1 garlic clove, chopped

1 green bell pepper, seeded and cut into strips

1 tsp each paprika, ground coriander, and ground cumin

$1/4$–$1/2$ tsp chili powder

14 oz/400 g canned chopped tomatoes

$2/3$ cup vegetable stock

1 tbsp tomato paste

14 oz/400 g canned red kidney beans, drained and rinsed

salt and pepper

2 tbsp chopped fresh cilantro

Thai Shrimp & Mushroom Rice

Dried Chinese mushrooms have a particularly intense flavor. If they are unavailable use any other dried mushrooms.

1 Place the mushrooms in a bowl, pour over enough boiling water to cover, and let soak for 30 minutes. Drain and chop.

2 Meanwhile, rinse the rice in several changes of water and drain thoroughly. Place in a pan with the water. Bring to a boil and stir once. Reduce the heat to a gentle simmer, then cover the pan and cook for 12 minutes, or until the rice is cooked and the water has been absorbed. Fluff the rice up with a fork.

3 Heat the oil in a preheated wok. Add the onion and garlic and cook, stirring occasionally, until soft. Add the chilies and stir-fry for 2 minutes. Stir in the bamboo shoots, mushrooms, and fish sauce.

4 Continue to stir-fry for 2 minutes, then stir in the rice and shrimp. Stir gently for a few minutes until completely heated through. Stir in the cilantro and serve at once.

SERVES 4

PREPARATION TIME: 15 MINUTES, PLUS 30 MINUTES SOAKING

COOKING TIME: 25 MINUTES

8 pieces dried Chinese black mushrooms

scant 1 cup long-grain white rice

1$\frac{1}{2}$ cups water

2 tbsp oil

1 small onion, finely chopped

2 garlic cloves, finely chopped

2 fresh red chilies, seeded and cut into thin strips

3 oz/85 g bamboo shoots, cut into short thin sticks

1 tbsp Thai fish sauce

6 oz/175 g cooked shelled shrimp

2 tbsp chopped fresh cilantro

Mushroom & Sage Risotto

Be careful not to overcook the risotto. The rice should be tender with a slightly soupy consistency—add extra liquid, if necessary.

1 Place the mushrooms in a bowl and cover with the water. Let soak for 15 minutes. Drain the mushrooms and strain the liquid into a pan. Pour in the stock and heat. Let simmer gently to keep it hot.

2 Heat half the butter in a large, heavy-bottom pan. Add the onion and garlic and cook gently for 10 minutes, until soft.

3 Add the dried and fresh mushrooms and cook for a few minutes until just soft. Stir in the white wine. Boil rapidly until reduced by one-third, then add the rice and sage. Stir in the hot stock, a little at a time, and wait until it has been absorbed before adding more.

4 Continue until all the stock has been added and the liquid has been absorbed. Stir in the remaining butter, salt and pepper to taste, and the Parmesan cheese and serve at once.

SERVES 4

PREPARATION TIME: 15 MINUTES, PLUS 15 MINUTES SOAKING

COOKING TIME: 30 MINUTES

2 tbsp dried porcini mushrooms

1$^1/_4$ cups hot water

3$^1/_2$ cups vegetable stock

3 oz/85 g butter

1 onion, finely chopped

2 garlic cloves, chopped

7 oz/200 g mixed wild mushrooms

$^2/_3$ cup dry white wine

generous 1$^1/_2$ cups risotto rice

1 tbsp chopped fresh sage

salt and pepper

$^1/_2$ cup freshly grated Parmesan cheese

Phyllo Mushroom Purses

SERVES 6 AS AN APPETIZER

PREPARATION TIME: 20 MINUTES, PLUS
20 MINUTES COOLING

COOKING TIME: 25 MINUTES

5 tbsp oil

4 oz/115 g white mushrooms, sliced

2 celery stalks, cut into thin shreds

1 carrot, cut into thin shreds

4 scallions, cut into thin shreds

1-inch/2.5-cm piece fresh gingerroot,
    grated

juice of 1 small lemon

salt and pepper

5 large sheets phyllo pastry, about
    18 x 12 inches/45 x 30 cm each

Check the phyllo purses toward the end of the cooking time.
If they are becoming too brown, cover lightly with waxed paper.

1 Heat 2 tablespoons of the oil in a large skillet. Add the
mushrooms, celery, carrot, scallions, and ginger and
stir-fry over high heat for 3–4 minutes, or until starting
to soften.

2 Add the lemon juice and stir-fry until the vegetables are
tender and the moisture has evaporated. Season to taste
with salt and pepper, then let cool. Preheat the oven
to 400°F/200°C.

3 Cut the pastry sheets into 4 pieces to make 20 rectangles.
Lightly brush each piece with oil and layer them in 6 piles of
3 pieces. There will be 2 pieces left over. These can be used
for patching any damaged pastry.

4 Divide the vegetable mixture between the 6 pastry rectangles,
draw up the pastry round the filling, and pinch the tops
together. Place on a baking sheet and brush with oil. Bake
for 20 minutes, until browned and crisp.

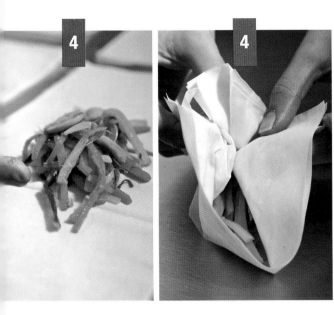

Mushroom & Taleggio Tarts

SERVES 4

PREPARATION TIME: 20 MINUTES, PLUS
30 MINUTES CHILLING

COOKING TIME: 50 MINUTES

1 lb/450 g ready-made puff pastry

all-purpose flour, for dusting

5 tbsp olive oil, plus extra for brushing

1 lb 9 oz/700 g red onions, thinly sliced

9 oz/250 g cremini mushrooms, sliced

2 tbsp pine nuts

1 tbsp chopped fresh oregano

salt and pepper

3¹/₂ oz/100 g Taleggio cheese, sliced

These tarts are easy to make as the puff pastry rises up round the filling, forming a pastry shell.

1 Roll out the pastry on a floured counter and cut out 4 x 5-inch/13 cm squares. Let chill for 30 minutes. Place 2 baking sheets in the oven and preheat the oven to 425°F/220°C.

2 Meanwhile, heat 3 tbsp of the oil in a skillet. Add the onions and cook gently for 30 minutes, until caramelized. Remove from the skillet and let cool.

3 Heat the remaining oil in the skillet. Add the mushrooms and cook over high heat until soft and the liquid has evaporated. Let cool, then stir into the onions. Mix in the pine nuts, oregano, and salt and pepper.

4 Place the chilled pastry squares on the baking sheets. Prick the pastry squares with a fork and brush with oil. Divide the mushroom mixture between them, leaving a ¹/₂-inch/1-cm margin. Arrange the cheese on the top. Bake for 15 minutes, until the pastry is golden and risen, and the cheese has melted.

Mushroom Stroganoff

SERVES 4

PREPARATION TIME: 5 MINUTES

COOKING TIME: 15 MINUTES

1 onion

2 tbsp butter

1 lb/450 g closed cup mushrooms

1 tsp tomato paste

1 tsp coarse grain mustard

2/3 cup sour cream

1 tsp paprika

salt and pepper

chopped fresh parsley, to garnish

This dish could be served with rice as a main dish or as an accompaniment to steak, chicken, or chops.

1 Chop the onion finely. Heat the butter in a large, heavy-bottom skillet. Add the onion and cook gently for 5–10 minutes, until soft. Meanwhile, trim and quarter the mushrooms.

2 Add the mushrooms to the skillet and stir-fry for a few minutes until they start to soften. Stir in the tomato paste and mustard, then add the sour cream. Cook gently, stirring constantly, for 5 minutes.

3 Stir in the paprika and season to taste with salt and pepper. Garnish with chopped parsley and serve at once.

Garlic Mushrooms

SERVES 4

PREPARATION TIME: 10 MINUTES

COOKING TIME: 20 MINUTES

1 lb/450 g medium cup mushrooms

6 oz/175 g softened butter

2 garlic cloves, crushed

juice and grated rind of ½ lemon

2 tbsp chopped fresh parsley

salt and pepper

fresh crusty bread, to serve

Serve these mushrooms with plenty of crusty bread to mop up the delicious garlicky juices.

1 Preheat the oven to 425°F/220°C. Remove the mushroom stalks and arrange the mushrooms, rounded-side down, in a shallow ovenproof dish.

2 Mix the butter, garlic, lemon juice and rind, parsley, salt, and pepper together in a bowl. Divide the garlic butter between the mushroom cups.

3 Bake in the oven for 15–20 minutes, until the mushrooms are soft and the garlic butter is sizzling. Serve at once with crusty bread.

Mushroom Fajitas

These fajitas can be as hot and spicy as you like according to the amount of cayenne pepper you use!

1 Cut the mushrooms into strips. Heat the oil in a large, heavy-bottom skillet. Add the mushrooms, onion, red and green bell pepper, and garlic and stir-fry for 8–10 minutes, until the vegetables are cooked.

2 Add the cayenne pepper, lime juice and rind, sugar, and oregano. Season to taste with salt and pepper and cook for an additional 2 minutes.

3 Meanwhile, heat the tortillas according to the package instructions. Divide the mushroom mixture between the warmed tortillas and serve with sour cream and salsa.

SERVES 4–8

PREPARATION TIME: 15 MINUTES

COOKING TIME: 12 MINUTES

1 lb 2 oz/500 g large flat mushrooms

2 tbsp oil

1 onion, sliced

1 red bell pepper, seeded and sliced

1 green bell pepper, seeded and sliced

1 garlic clove, crushed

$1/4$–$1/2$ tsp cayenne pepper

juice and grated rind of 2 limes

2 tsp sugar

1 tsp dried oregano

salt and pepper

8 flour tortillas

To serve

sour cream

salsa

Index

Make and Use

Books

Anna-Marie D'Cruz

WAYLAND

First published in 2007
by Wayland

© Copyright 2007 Wayland

Wayland
338 Euston Road
London NW1 3BH

Wayland Australia
Level 17/207 Kent Street
Sydney NSW 2000

Senior Editor: Jennifer Schofield
Designer: Jason Billin
Project maker: Anna-Marie D'Cruz
Photographer: Chris Fairclough
Proofreader: Susie Brooks

Acknowledgements:
The Publishers would like to thank the following models:
Emel Augustin, Jade Campbell, Ammar Duffus, Akash Kohli,
Ellie Lawrence, Katie Powell, Eloise Ramplin, Robin Stevens

Picture Credits:
All photography by Chris Fairclough except for
page 4 top Brooklyn Museum/CORBIS; Page 4 bottom CORBIS;
page 7 Bob Krist/CORBIS;

CIP data
D'Cruz, Anna-Marie
   Books. - (Make and use)
   1. Book design - Juvenile literature
   I. Title
   741.6

ISBN: 9 7807 5025 055 9

Printed in China

Wayland is a division of Hachette Children's Books.

Note to parents and teachers:
The projects in this book are designed to be made by children. However, we do recommend adult supervision at all times as the Publisher cannot be held responsible for any injury caused while making the projects.

Contents

All about books

We read and use books all the time, from storybooks and notebooks to address books and telephone directories. But books as we know them have changed a lot since they were first made.

BOOKS AND WRITING

Books are linked to the start of writing. As long ago as 10000BCE in China and the Middle East, people wrote things down on clay and later on wax. In about 2500BCE, the Ancient Egyptians used papyrus to make a type of paper (see right). Papyrus is a reed that grows next to water. The leaves of the plant were pressed and dried to make the papyrus, which could be used like a piece of paper.

Today's books are all printed on huge printing presses, but this has not always been the case. In about 700CE, the Chinese invented a type of printing – woodblock printing. They carved out letters from blocks of wood and then covered them with ink. The inky blocks were then pressed down onto paper – similar to using a stamp – so that the letters were printed on the page. A major change in printing took place in about 1438, when Germany's Johannes Gutenberg invented the printing press. In 1455 Gutenberg used his press to print a Bible (see left).

TODAY'S BOOKS

Books come in all sorts of different styles, sizes and shapes. The process of putting a book together is known as bookbinding. Books can be bound in different ways – for example, the pages can be stitched or stapled to keep them together or they can be glued. Books usually have a cover to protect the inside pages. The covers need to be strong and are often made from materials, such as cardboard, wood and leather.

Books can be used for many different things. They can provide information such as an encyclopedia, dictionary or atlas, or they can be used to keep records of things, as in an address book or a notebook.

GET STARTED!

In this book, there are projects for creating many different kinds of book. When you make your books, try to use materials that you already have either at home or at school. For example, instead of buying cardboard, the backs of used-up notepads, writing pads, art pads and hardbacked envelopes are ideal. Reusing and recycling materials like this is good for the environment and it saves you money. The projects have all been made and decorated for this book, but do not worry if yours look a little different – just have fun making them.

Badge holder

Fabric is great for making books because it is strong and can be washed. In this project you can make your own fabric book for keeping your favourite badges safe.

1 Cut one large, one medium and one small rectangle from the felt. If you have a pair of pinking shears then use these instead of scissors as they give a zig-zag effect.

2 Lay the rectangles on top of each other, with the largest one at the bottom and the smallest one at the top. Staple them together down the middle.

3 Fold the end of one length of ribbon over and staple it halfway up the side of the front cover of the book. Do the same with the other length of ribbon, this time stapling it to the back cover. Be careful not to staple the pages together.

4 To decorate the front cover, cut out and glue on shapes of felt.

FAB FELT

Felt is a fabric made from wool. This means that it is good for making hats and clothes that keep you warm. It is used in Mongolia, where it is extremely cold, to make tents known as yurts.

5 You can now start pinning your badges to the felt pages to keep your collection safe.

Folding book

Folding books were first used in Thailand and Myanmar. They were made from long sheets of paper which were folded into zig-zag shapes. Follow these steps to make your own folding book. If you like, you can decorate it with symbols of the Chinese zodiac.

YOU WILL NEED

A4 sheet of red card

ruler

pencil

pair of scissors

glue

coloured artfoam

square of corrugated card, 9cm x 9cm

newspaper

paint and paintbrush

green card, 2 9cm x 9cm

2 squares of stiff card, 9cm x 9cm

12 squares of yellow paper, 5cm x 5cm

coloured pencils

elastic band

1 Measure out and cut three strips of red card that are 7cm wide and the length of the card. Stick the strips together, overlapping each end by 1.5cm, to make one long strip.

2 Fold one end of the strip of card over by 7cm. Then fold it back the other way, also by 7cm. Continue folding backwards and forwards to create a zig-zag. Trim off any extra card.

3 To make a stamp to decorate the book's cover, cut out a shape from the artfoam – we have used a Chinese symbol. Flip the shape over so that it is reversed. Then glue the shape to the square of corrugated card.

4 Cover your work surface with newspaper. To make the book covers, brush paint onto the stamp and press it onto one of the green squares of card. Repeat the print on the other green square. Glue the green squares onto the squares of stiff card.

5 Glue the back of one of the covers to the end of the red zig-zag. Fold up the zig-zag and glue the second cover to the other end. Make sure your cover is the correct way up!

6 Onto the twelve yellow squares, draw pictures or write a story. Glue one yellow square onto each page.

CHINESE ZODIAC

In China, each year is symbolised by a different animal. These are the rat, bull, tiger, rabbit, dragon, snake, horse, sheep, monkey, rooster, dog and pig. Try to find out which animal represents the year in which you were born.

7 When the glue has dried, close the book and place an elastic band around it to hold it closed.

Palm-leaf book

Palm-leaf books get their name because their pages were traditionally made from the leaves of palm trees. The books had wooden covers to protect their pages. Make your own palm-leaf-style book and use it to record your favourite recipe.

1 To make the pages, measure ten strips of 21cm x 2cm from the green card. Cut them out.

YOU WILL NEED

A4 sheet of green card
ruler
pen or pencil
pair of scissors
hole punch
A4 sheet of black card
glue
metallic pens
1m of cord
2 beads that will thread onto the cord

2 Measure 10.5cm from the edge of each strip and make a mark. Use this to position a hole punch so that the holes will be in the same place on each strip. Punch holes in the card.

3 For the covers, cut two rectangles measuring 21cm x 4cm from the black card. Fold each one in half along the length and glue the insides together. Punch holes in the same position as in the green strips. Use the metallic pens to decorate each cover.

4 Thread the cord ends through the holes on the decorated side of one cover. Then thread on the pages one by one, finishing with the other cover, with the decorated side on the outside.

5 Tie a double knot about 10cm in from the end of each cord. Thread on a bead and tie a knot just above it.

6 Spread the 'leaves' and write down your recipe. Then gather the pages together and tie the cord around them for safe keeping.

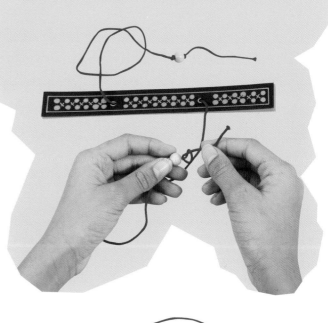

Scrambled eggs

Ingredients: 2 eggs, 1 tbs milk, salt, pepper,

knob of butter, toast to serve

Method: 1. Whisk together the eggs, milk,

salt, and pepper.

2. Melt the butter in a frying

pan until it starts to bubble.

3. Add the egg mixture and stir

RECIPES

A recipe is a set of instructions explaining how to cook something. Recipes usually have a list of what you need (the ingredients) and a set of instructions (the method).

Lift the flaps

In a lift-the-flap book, hidden areas on the pages are discovered by lifting a piece of paper. Why not write your own story for a lift-the-flap book?

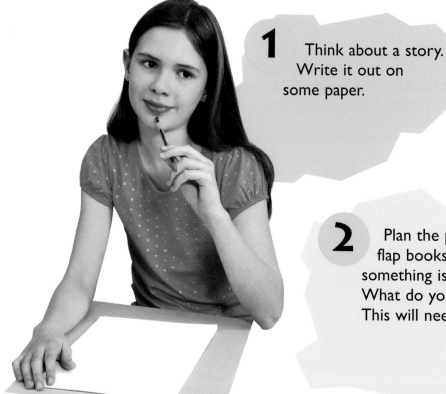

1 Think about a story. Write it out on some paper.

2 Plan the pictures for your story – lift-the-flap books work best with pictures where something is hiding or is inside something else. What do you want the flap to be hiding? This will need to be part of the main picture.

3 When you are happy with your story, draw the main picture onto one half of a clean sheet of white paper. The object being hidden needs to be part of this drawing.

4 Fold a sheet of coloured card in half. Cut out and paste the main picture onto one half of the card. Colour it in.

5 On another sheet of paper, make the flap by drawing the front of the hiding place. Colour it in and cut it out. Stick your flap onto the main drawing.

6 Repeat steps one to five until you have drawn pictures for the whole story. Glue every two pages back to back and staple all the pages together when you are finished to make a book.

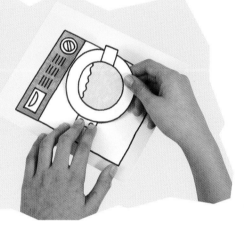

What is in the washing machine?

What is behind the door?

What is in the washing machine?

What is behind the door?

Pop-up book

A pop-up book is always full of surprises. Each time you turn a page, something will spring out at you. Follow these steps to make a simple pop-up.

YOU WILL NEED

A4 sheets of coloured card

permanent marker

ruler

pencil

pair of scissors

colouring pencils

glue

1 Fold a sheet of coloured card in half. Draw on two horizontal lines from the folded edge which are 5cm long.

2 Cut along the lines. Bend back the middle section, as shown.

3 Open up your card and push the cut shape inwards. Close your card and press it flat. Open the card again so that you have a pop-up rectangle.

4 Measure the width of your card, from the fold to the edge. This will tell you how wide your pop-up picture can be. If it is any wider then your picture will stick out of the side when the page is closed.

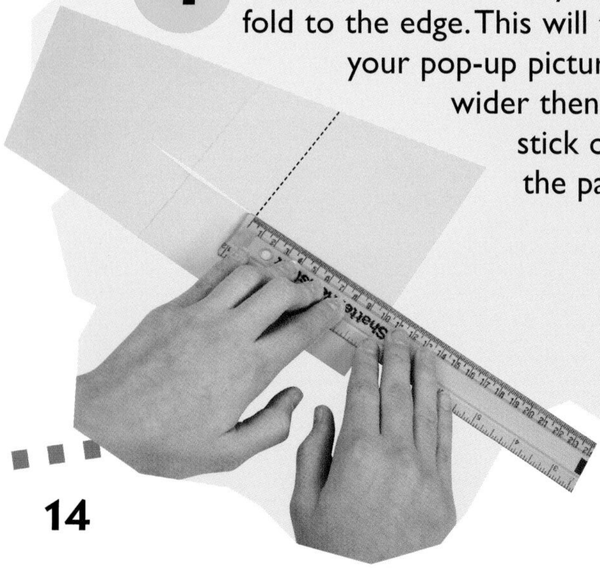

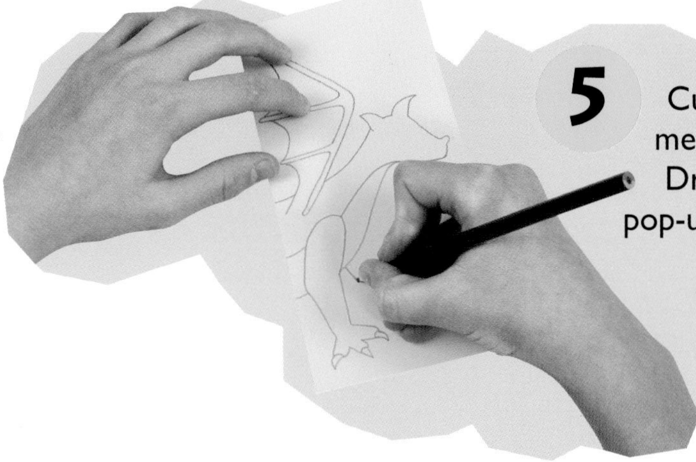

5 Cut another piece of card as wide as the measurement from step 4 and 21cm high. Draw what you want to be on your pop-up onto this card.

6 Colour in the drawing, cut it out and glue it to the pop-up rectangle. You could make more than one pop-up on the same-sized card and glue each one together. Write your story below the pictures.

MORE POP-UPS

The shape of the pop-up can vary, as shown below. Experiment with different shapes by changing the way you make the cut in steps 1 and 2.

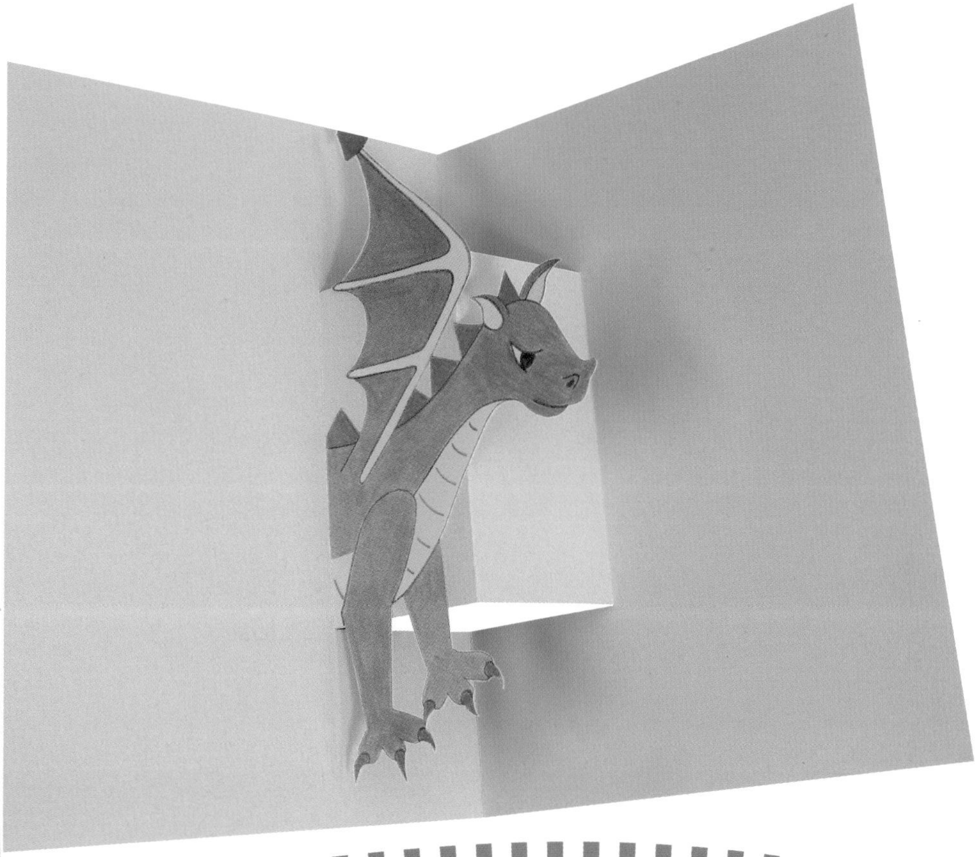

Address book

To make an alphabetical address book, you need to use tabs. The tabs allow you to quickly turn to the pages you want. Put a hardback cover on your book to protect the pages.

YOU WILL NEED

- 8 A4 sheets of paper
- stapler
- pencil
- ruler
- pair of scissors
- eraser
- 2 pieces of card,
  15 x 22cm
- 1 strip of card,
  0.5cmx 22cm
- sheet of wrapping paper,
  36cm x 26cm
- glue
- pen

1 Fold all your sheets of paper in half to make a crease. Unfold the paper but, keeping the pages together, staple down the crease and fold.

2 To make the tabs, use a pencil and ruler to draw a line down the right-hand side of the third page, about 2cm in from the edge. Lightly mark off 13 equal lengths (each about 1.6cm) on this line.

3 Cut the third page from the bottom up to the top mark to leave a tab at the top. Cut the next page up to the second mark so that it appears beneath the top tab. Do the same for each sheet, each time cutting up to the next mark down, until you end up with 13 tabs. Rub out any pencil marks.

4 To add the cover, glue the card shapes onto the back of the wrapping paper, as shown. The gap between the spine and covers needs to be at least 0.5cm.

5 Glue and fold over the top and bottom. Then glue and fold in the sides, pressing down firmly.

6 Take your tabbed pages and put glue on the front page. Stick this to the centre of the inside front cover. Put glue on the back page and stick it down.

7 Write the alphabet in pairs of letters down the side on the tabs. The address book is now ready to use.

EF
GH
IJ
KL
MN
OP
QR
ST
UV
WX
YZ

photo album

A photo album is a book for displaying photographs and keeping them safe. Make your own album to hold your favourite family photographs. You could decorate the cover with your family tree.

YOU WILL NEED

5 A4 sheets of coloured paper
pair of scissors
5 A4 sheets of tracing paper
A4 sheet of coloured card
21cm x 15cm reused card
23cm x 15cm reused card
glue
hole punch
coloured paper for decorating
2 paper fasteners (split pins)

1 Cut the 5 sheets of coloured paper in half across the width to give you 10 sheets. Do the same with the tracing paper.

2 Cut the sheet of coloured card in half and glue it onto the two rectangles of reused card to hide any writing or pictures. On the longer cover, not all of the print or pictures will be hidden.

3 Punch holes in all the sheets of paper and in the covers, in the middle of one of the short edges. Make sure the holes are in the same place on each page. For the longer cover the holes should be along the uncovered edge. Fold the covers on the holed side about 2cm in from the edge.

4 Turn over the shorter cover and decorate it. You could cut out a tree trunk and branch shape from coloured paper and glue them down. Cut circles of card and glue them down onto the ends of the branches. Write the names of people in your family onto the circles.

5 To bind the photo album together, put the front cover face down, placing the holes over two unopened paper fasteners. Take it in turns to place a sheet of tracing paper and then coloured paper over the fasteners.

6 Place the longer cover over the fasteners, sticking out the opposite way from the pile of pages. Make sure the coloured card is facing downwards. Open up the fasteners and fold the card over the book to finish the back cover.

7 Your album is now ready for photographs. You can add more sheets if you need to by removing the back cover.

FAMILY TREES

A family tree is a chart showing how different members of a family are connected. They can also give information of when people were born and died, where they lived and what they did for work. They can tell you a lot about your family history.

Brian Julie Keith Nicola
John Mary Katie
Adam Peter
Sue

Eco-notebook

Making your own paper is a great way to recycle bits of old newspaper. Put together sheets of handmade paper to make an environmentally friendly notebook.

YOU WILL NEED

4 long lollipop sticks
4 elastic bands
pair of clean, old tights
pair of scissors
newspaper torn into small pieces plus 1 extra newspaper
plastic basin
5 pints of warm tap water
balloon whisk
2 old face flannels
rolling pin
hole punch
string

1 To make a frame, lay the lollipop sticks in a square shape and wrap the elastic bands tightly around the corners. You will need a frame for each sheet of paper you make.

2 Cut off a length from a leg of the tights and pull it over the frame to make a screen.

3 Put the torn pieces of newspaper into the basin with the warm water. Allow the paper to soak for about three hours. Then use the whisk to mash up the paper. Keep resting the mixture and whisking again until you have a grey 'pulp' that looks like thick soup. This may take a while so be patient!

4 For a blotting surface, lay half of the spare newspaper down and place one of the flannels on top. Keep the rest of the newspaper and the other flannel nearby.

5 Slide the frame into the basin, wriggling it around to get an even layer of pulp onto your screen. Pull up the frame, keeping it as level as possible. Allow the water to drip through into the basin. Lay the frame onto the blotting surface.

6 Cover the frame with the other flannel. Put the remaining newspaper over the flannel. Use the rolling pin to squeeze out as much water as possible.

7 Lift up the top part of the blotter. Lift off the frame and leave it to dry. When it is dry, carefully peel off the paper. Repeat steps 4 to 7 to make more paper. Trim the pages to neaten them up. Punch a hole in the paper, in the same place on each sheet, and tie the pages together with string to make a notebook.

REED PAPER

The Ancient Egyptians made a type of paper called papyrus. It was made from lengths of the papyrus reed which were placed side by side, and then another layer was put on top at right angles. The papyrus was then soaked, squeezed dry and hammered to flatten it into a thin sheet of 'paper'.

Glossary

alphabetical

When something is in the order of the alphabet – from A to Z.

binding

The way the pages in a book are held together. Some books are stitched down the middle while others are stapled or glued.

blotter

Something that soaks up water or other liquids.

Chinese Zodiac

The twelve animals that represent different years in the Chinese calendar.

environmentally friendly

When something is good for the environment or will not damage the Earth, it is environmentally friendly. Reusing and recycling are environmentally friendly.

felt

A thick type of fabric made from wool.

material

Anything used for making something else. Wool, wood, plastic and metal are all materials.

Middle East

The countries to the east of the Mediterranean Sea. The Middle East includes Egypt, Iraq and Iran.

Mongolia

A country in central Asia.

papyrus

A water plant that was used to make a type of paper in Ancient Egypt.

pinking shears

A special kind of scissors that cut zig-zags instead of straight lines.

printing press

A machine that can print thousands of copies of a document at once.

recipe

A set of instructions for cooking a particular dish of food. Recipes usually list the ingredients of the dish. They also have a method which tells you what to do and in what order to do it.

recycling

To recycle something is to change it or treat it so that it can be used again.

reusing

Using something for a different purpose. For example, if you use the cardboard from a cereal packet to make a project, you are reusing the cardboard.

right angle

An angle of 90 degrees. The corners of a rectangle and square are angled at 90 degrees.

tab

A small strip or flap that sticks out. Sometimes tabs are labelled with numbers or letters, depending on the information they store.

woodblock printing

A method of printing that started in China in about 700CE. Letters were carved into wood and 'stamped' onto paper.

yurts

A circle-shaped tent used by the nomads (people who move their homes about) of Mongolia.

FURTHER INFORMATION

www.makingbooks.com/freeprojects.shtml
   There are lots of fun book projects to make from this Website.
www.enchantedlearning.com/crafts/books
   This website has examples of many different types of books.
   Why not see if you can make some of them?
www.nationalgeographic.com/ngkids/0502/
   Lots of information on the Chinese Zodiac. You can find out which
   animal you are and how some people believe that this could influence your personality.
www.kidsturncentral.com/topics/hobbies/kidsgenealogy.htm
   This information-packed website will show you how to sort out your family tree.

Note to parents and teachers:

The website addresses (URLs) included in this book were valid at the time of going to press. However, because of the nature of the Internet, it is possible that some addresses may have changed, or sites may have changed or closed down since publication. While the author and publishers regret any inconvenience this may cause the readers, no responsibility for any such changes can be accepted by either the author or the publisher.

Index

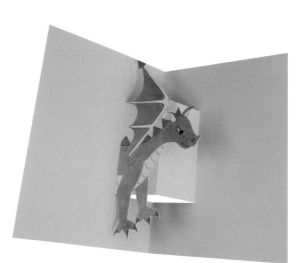